What Do We Do
NOW??

The Complete Guide for All New Parents and Parents-To-Be!

PAUL R. FEINSINGER

Illustrated by Suzanne Carroll Feinsinger

CCC Publications • Los Angeles

Published by

CCC Publications
20306 Tau Place
Chatsworth, CA 91311

Manufactured in the United States of America

Cover design © 1991 CCC Publications

Cover Art by Steve Gray

Illustrations © 1988 Paul R. Feinsinger

Illustrations © by Suzanne Carroll Feinsinger

ISBN:0-918259-18-5

First Printing - 1/89
Second Printing - 2/89
Third Printing - 11/89
Fourth Printing - 10/90
Fifth Printing - 5/91

If your local U.S. bookstore is out of stock, copies of this book may be obtained by mailing check or money order for $4.95 per book (plus $2.00 to cover postage and handling) to: CCC Publications; 20306 Tau Place; Chatsworth, CA 91311.

This book is dedicated to:

My parents, who were always telling me to clean up my room;
My wife, who is still telling me to clean up my room; and
My children, who never clean up their rooms.

With all my love to
Ashley, Rebecca and
Suzanne.

TABLE OF CONTENTS

PROLOGUE

There's an old story said to have taken place on Groucho Marx's "You Bet Your Life" television show. The show would feature contestants trying to win money by guessing the answers to questions from various categories. Before they got a shot at the money, the contestants were subjected to "on-the-air" inquiries about their personal lives. This particular inquiry went something like this . . .

> Groucho: *So, Mr. Jones, tell us about yourself.*
> Mr. Jones: *Well, Groucho, I have eleven children.*
> Groucho: *Eleven children! How do you account for this?*
> Mr. Jones: *Well, Groucho, I love my wife very much.*
> Groucho: *Well, I happen to like my cigar, but I take it out of my mouth once in a while!*

Eleven children! That's unbelievable, if not "inconceivable". If *you're* considering spawning that many kids, the following pages will convince you otherwise. As should any financial planner, your local public school system, the city garbage collectors, Santa Claus, your first born, your neighborhood, *Mrs.* Jones, members of Zero Population Growth, your babysitter, the family uterus, the executor of your will, anyone paying child support . . .

INTRODUCTION

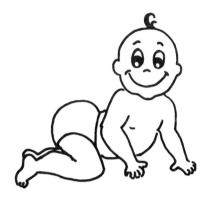

There's no owner's manual. No simple step-by-step instructions. No parts warranty (though labor is usually guaranteed for up to three days).

Yet, when this item is taken out of its packaging, you're supposed to know exactly what to do with it. After all, it's just another human being. And, there have been zillions of these running around for years.

So, raising a baby should be a snap, right? No problem, right? Piece o' cake, right?

Good luck.

CHAPTER 1

When You Know It's Time

It's the moment you've anticipated for nearly three-quarters of a year. The moment that marks the end of "radiance" and signals the beginning of "Oh, my God!"

Your baby is making its move.

But, before you allow panic to set in, you have to take some immediate action. First and foremost, no matter what time of day it is, get a good night's sleep. This will be your last chance for about three years. Next, if you haven't chosen a hospital yet, now's the time . . . but check your medical insurance first. While many policies permit you to have your baby at any participating hospital, the more economical plans will only provide reimbursement if you're treated by a retired veterinarian.

Regardless of where you're going to have your baby, you should make a complete list of everything you're going to need over the next few days. This list should include all of the following:

> 1. A threshold for pain never imagined by any living human being.

This is all you'll really need. Nothing else will

matter. Although a smart move would be to bring a suitcase full of extra underwear. (This will be deeply appreciated by those friends and relatives in the waiting room who have nervous bladders.)

When you arrive at the hospital, you'll have to stop at the Admitting Window. Here, the admitting clerk will ask you seemingly perfunctory questions which may assist the doctor in case there are any complications during the delivery. For example . . .

- Are you sure you're pregnant?
- Did you bring your checkbook?
- Are your next-of-kin coming, and are they bringing their checkbooks?

Next, you'll be taken by wheelchair (or forklift, depending upon your weight) toward the labor room. On your way, you'll pass a group of bubble-gum-smacking teen-aged girls who are huddled around a television watching MTV.

This is the nursing station.

One of these girls will be assigned to assist you during your labor — or during a commercial, whichever she feels like. Don't worry, she *is* a nurse. And, when things get serious, she'll be right at your side . . . watching MTV on the television in *your* room.

PEOPLE WHO WILL ASSIST
THE DOCTOR
WITH YOUR DELIVERY.

NURSE   SPOUSE

If you're lucky, you may be able to have your baby in what some hospitals call the "alternative birthing" room. This room is supposed to make you feel more relaxed because it doesn't have that stark labor room environment. Actually, the alternative birthing room is decorated more like your living room — dust on the window sills, crooked pictures on the wall and cigarette burns in the furniture all add that extra touch. Most hospitals permit you to have several friends come into this room so they can watch you have the baby. What makes the hospital think you have any friends who want to see this? Your friends are going to bolt for the toilet when you bring out the Polaroids of the blessed event two weeks later. Hey, the natural birth process has the baby coming from an area on your body where even *you* don't have to watch. This is no accident. If nature had intended mothers to watch their babies being born, you'd be delivering your baby through your nose! (The scary part is, with some people, this looks entirely possible.)

Regardless of which room you choose, you're going to be in for some "no-kidding" labor stuff and your contractions are going to become quite painful. How you deal with that pain can make all the difference in the world. (Okay, so it probably won't make any difference at all, but here are some suggestions anyway.)

4

1. Do Proper Breathing. Many mothers have chosen the "Lamaze" or similar breathing techniques to help them get through the tougher parts of labor. However, a great percentage of these mothers have said that it didn't really help. The pain was still unbearable. If that's the case, you should try a different breathing technique. The "*No* Breathing" technique. Just hold your breath until you pass out. For the rest of your labor you won't feel a thing and your spouse/coach can wile away the time by playing a few rounds of gin rummy with the waiting room crowd.

2. Put Your Mind Elsewhere. Think of something serene and less painful than your labor — like the Soviet Union's entire nuclear arsenal dropping on your house. (If that's so far-fetched you can't effectively concentrate, make it only half their arsenal and throw in a broken fingernail.)

3. Get Out the "Yellow Pages". Look under "Emergency Surrogates".

Soon the pain will become excruciating, and, what's worse, you'll still have h-o-u-r-s to go. From down the hall, you'll hear frightening screams that will conjure up all sorts of horrifying images of what another mommy-to-be is going through, and what you've yet to experience. More likely, though, it's

Emergency Sermons 555-1020
Emergency Soul Food 555-6903
Emergency Spaying 555-8822

Emergency Stoolpigeons 555-7584
Emergency Suction Cups 555-3663
Emergency Surfboards 555-5555

EMERGENCY SURROGATE

"The Labor Lady"

Licensed
and has Bonded!

Ask About our
Special Discount
for Twins!

We Deliver!
555-HELP

coming from one of the part-time LVNs who just found out she has to work her second straight Saturday night. And you think you've got problems.

After what seems like months (it's really only weeks), the doctor will arrive, casually dressed, carrying your chart — and sporting a 9-iron. This will tend to make you a bit nervous wondering just how he plans to deliver your baby. Relax. From where your baby is positioned, there's no way he can get to it using that club. He needs a 5-iron at least. Unless his plan is to wait for the baby to get "closer to the hole".

"How are we doing?" the doctor will inquire.

Ask him how *he'd* be doing if a logging truck were trying to drive its way out of his body — through his rear end. The doctor will then turn and gingerly walk out of the room. And he will never ask you another stupid question as long as he lives.

CHAPTER 2

What To Do The Moment The Baby Is Born

Many couples experience a tremendous letdown the moment their baby is born. What with no more pain, screaming, torture and other "fruits of labor", the immediate post-natal time period can be very boring.

But, you can avoid this anti-climactic lull by planning something your baby will never forget.

Plan to throw your newborn a surprise party!

Now, before you toss off this idea as absurd, consider the advantages:

— To make the "surprise" work, your guests will not have to park their cars around the corner from the hospital because baby will not be arriving from the same entrance.

— The list of invitees can be kept to a minimum (after all, the only things baby has known up to this point are thousands of micro-organisms floating around in mommy's stomach and, chances are, only a few of them will be able to attend on such short notice).

REFRAIN FROM PLAYING PRACTICAL JOKES
ON YOUR BABY FOR AT LEAST 48 HOURS.
OTHERWISE, YOUR BABY WILL GROW UP
TO BE JUST LIKE EDDIE HASKELL.

Like any other surprise party, though, this one requires careful preparation. If you still have time, notify the hospital that you'd like the delivery room decorated (tastefully) with streamers and balloons. Order party favors and hats for the nurses. Pre-select traditional birthday party favorites like cookies and punch. Perhaps mommy can have a crayon drawing of the Kool-Aid Man's face rendered on her breast so baby can feel included in the festivities. (NOTE: Don't leave this for the last minute. Most doctors and nurses do not have a particularly good artist's hand, much less a variety of Crayolas in the delivery room.)

Jot down some party games that will keep these first few minutes of baby's life interesting. "Pin the Umbilical Cord on the Doctor" is always a crowd-pleaser, as is a mother/daughter potato sack race. The latter, of course, depends heavily upon the baby's gender, and partially upon mommy's condition.

Naturally, the key to pulling off any surprise party is secrecy. You and your spouse can never mention a word about it, because babies, while still in the womb, can hear everything. This is how they know which family members to hate from the moment they're born.

With all the preparations in order, and you're close to the big moment — about three to five minutes before baby's grand entrance — have a pre-assigned nurse turn out the lights in the delivery room. This makes everything more suspenseful . . . including the doctor's ability to successfully complete the delivery. Another nurse should then say, "Sh-h-h! Quiet everybody! Here it comes!" When the doctor says "Okay", and you're satisfied that he's holding your baby and not one of his shoes, have the nurse flick on the lights. Everybody yell "Surprise!"

If baby immediately starts to cry, it knew about the party all along. And, at this early stage in your relationship, you'll realize that, from now on, no matter what you try to do for your kid, it will never be good enough.

CHAPTER 3
After The Delivery

When the delivery is complete, you'll get your first look at your new baby. You'll marvel in wonderment at how this human being grew and developed in mommy's stomach, especially when you consider all the submarine sandwiches, Hostess Snowballs and other gastro-intestinal meteorites this kid had to dodge for the better part of a year.

If you had a Caesarean delivery, your baby will look perfect — nice, round face, roly-poly arms and legs, cute behind. If you delivered by natural childbirth, your baby's head is going to look like a banana. This only lasts a few days, however, unless "banana heads" is a family trait. Assuming the two of you have normal cranial shapes, but your baby's still looks like a banana when you get home, put up fun-house mirrors in every room so the little "Chiquita" doesn't develop a psychological problem.

When you're through in the delivery room, it's off to the recovery room. Here, mommy will remain for a couple of hours — or as long as daddy needs to recover.

In the waiting room, friends and relatives will be making all sorts of embarrassing noises as they've begun the slow process of peeling their skin away from the naugahyde furniture where they've been affixed for the past 83 hours.

And, your baby is on its way to the nursery.

Before baby can enter the nursery, however, a bracelet will be given or footprints will be taken so your baby can be properly identified. In hospitals located in the more affluent parts of town, your baby can merely show a major credit card as an acceptable form of I.D.

After your baby has been in the nursery for several minutes, it will tune in to the cries of all the other babies. Listening intently for a moment, your baby will be able to find its niche, selecting a cry that's distinctly its own. The nurse will listen to your baby's "crying application", and, if she feels your baby's chosen an available wail, she'll issue an "official crying license". This license is irrevocable and is valid until the date of your child's second birthday . . . when it automatically converts into a "tantrum permit". Tantrum permits generally expire after about a year, but can be extended if you can annually prove to a "tantrum review board" that your child still needs one. John McEnroe's parents hold the record for extensions.

As early as a few days after the delivery, mommies may find themselves going into a deep depression. They'll feel as if the world is collapsing on their shoulders and begin to sob uncontrollably. This is

known as "post-partum blues". Daddies may also experience these same symptoms.

This is known as getting the hospital bill.

Be forewarned. Many hospitals will not release your baby until you have paid for it — in full. And, there are no returns either. You can't just pay for the baby, take it with you and then decide you don't like it. What would you say to the doctor? "Well, it looked good in the womb, but when I got it home, it really wasn't me." Sorry, folks. The hospital is running a business. This is an "all-sales-final" purchase. You can plead all you want, but they absolutely will not give you your money back. This is the reason many of today's modern-thinking parents are choosing to have their babies at Sears.

With all the commotion over paying the bill, you'll not want to forget to take a few things with you when it's time to leave, like . . .

1. Your baby. Don't laugh. It wasn't in your hands when you walked in.

2. The bent steel bedrails from the labor room. These will serve as helpful reminders when you're deciding whether you should have another baby.

3. The hospital towels. Since your bill will approximate the cost of three weeks at a four-star hotel, feel free to take the towels as souvenirs. In fact, if you can lift it, take the TV, too.

Although these items serve their purpose, they don't begin to prepare you for what you're going to need when you get home. If you're not real sure about the right things to buy, you're in trouble. And, the advertising business knows it. Interested only in making an extra buck, this industry preys upon your ignorance. For instance, witness disposable diaper commercials. They show someone putting a dropper-full of quick-drying liquid that wouldn't leak through one-ply toilet paper onto their diaper and call it "super absorbent". Who do they think they're kidding? You want to do the test *right?* Take one of those diapers and get yourself a firehose!!

How about those baby shampoos that claim "no more tears"? Folks, you haven't *seen* tears until you try to wash a baby's hair! Perhaps the best example is that happy-go-lucky, smiling infant on the jar of baby spinach. Say what you will, but that kid is lying through its gums. Nobody eats that crap and comes away smiling.

So that you don't feel that you're being left to the advertising buzzards, the following is a checklist of items that you'll need to have at home immediately upon your arrival:

1. A comfortable pair of shoes. With the amount of "up-all-night-holding-the-baby" walking you'll be doing, these will be essential. For those of you with fussy babies, consider buying a *dozen* pairs. For those of you with *colicky* babies, you'll need a collection rivaling that of Imelda Marcos.

2. A safety razor. Daddies with a moustache and/or beard will want to instantly shave them off. Babies love to grab this hair in a playful attempt to yank the skin off your face. (NOTE: If mommy also needs a razor for the same reason, the two of you had no business creating a child in the first place.)

3. A very large pacifier. For your mother, when she begins mouthing off about everything you're doing wrong with your baby. For the more serious cases, add a touch of "Krazy Glue" to the pacifier's tip.

4. A change of address form. File this immediately with the post office. Put down some phony address in another state. This is your only hope of controlling the deluge of baby junk mail solicitations already headed your way.

5. A medicine ball (mommies only). By practicing with this for just a few hours a day, within two weeks you'll be able to swiftly and accurately launch your baby at daddy when he comes home from work. This is known as the "here-it's-your-turn" baby pass.

6. A chest protector (daddies only). See number 5.

7. A rectal thermometer. To be used when your baby is screaming and thrashing unconsolably, and your pediatrician's answering service operator demands that you take the baby's temperature before she'll even consider connecting you to the doctor. You can send this to her (with absolutely no Vaseline), politely suggesting what she can do with it.

CHAPTER 4

How To Cope After You've Carried Baby Across The Threshold

Well, you made it. The two of you endured nine long, arduous months — not to mention the pleasures of labor and delivery. And, the fun is just beginning! Because now you have the menial job of raising a baby. Another human being for which the two of you are totally responsible. Yet, all the books in the world (except this one, of course) can't begin to prepare you for what lies ahead — partially because a great deal of it is unknown; and what *is* known, you don't want to know. But, take solace in knowing that somehow, some way, you'll manage. Lots of other people have. Those who *couldn't* manage, killed themselves. So you'll manage.

As the two of you bring baby into your home, you'll notice that this is the first time in nearly three months that mommy can fit through the interior doorways without soaping up the door jambs and having daddy push from behind. This has immediate positive results as you will now be more punctual when you are going out. Unfortunately, you won't be going out.

19

The next thing you'll notice is that your house is probably, and understandably, a mess. While mommy was in the hospital, daddy was doing his part by turning the house into a veritable disaster area. Tons of newspapers, soiled laundry and fast-food bags can be found in any room, while ketchup-stained paper plates are stacked up in the sink — a clever way to avoid doing the dishes *and* taking out the trash!

The good news is you're going to have company — by the droves. But, with daddy most likely having to return to work, and mommy too fatigued to do much of anything, don't worry for a moment about what your home looks like. Your company is coming to see the new baby, not your living room. They won't say anything about the untidy appearance — at least not to you. Once they leave, they'll talk about gathering support for a petition that requires you to give up the baby because "no infant should be brought up in that mess", and how the two of you are "obviously not ready for the responsibilities of parenthood". But this will blow over in a few years and you'll be able to keep your child.

One room you'll want to give a little attention to is the baby's nursery. But, be careful. It's very easy to go overboard with this room's decorations, and without realizing it, you can quickly spend thousands of dollars trying to make the nursery a shrine to "cuteness". The stores sucker you into buying coordinated, miniature wicker furniture, designer "duckie" wallpaper, Mother Goose lampshades, Care Bear crib sheets, teddy bear bumper guards, Yogi Bear curtains, mobiles with birdies, mobiles with beagles, mobiles with bunnies, Winnie-the-Pooh switchplates, Humpty-Dumpty doorstops, and the list goes on and on, *"add infant-item"*. No one really knows where this over-indulgent mentality came from. Back when *you* were a baby, droppers-by would "ooh" and "aah" if your nursery consisted of orange-colored dresser drawer knobs and a tattered Raggedy Ann doll propped up against a Felix-the-Cat diaper pail. And you only got those because your parents were resourceful enough to send a few boxtops to some warehouse in Battle Creek, Michigan.

As the first few weeks pass, you'll be carefully watching your baby's development. How it moves, sleeps, responds to stimuli, etc. For instance, did you know that most babies will remain alert for only about 3% of daylight hours? For a quick parallel of this statistic, that's about half of what's required of a clerk at the Department of Motor Vehicles.

Also, at the age of about one month, your baby may be able to lift its head approximately 45 degrees, babble something, then clumsily slam its head back down. You'll quickly recognize this sequence of movement as what you normally do on New Year's morning.

"ACTUALLY, THIS IS THE MASTER BEDROOM.
WE RAN OUT OF ROOM IN THE NURSERY!"

Dog/Cat/Baby Comparison Chart

	Dog	Cat	Baby
— Needs to go to Obedience School			✔
— Will eat 25¢ baby food	✔	✔	
— Will like you for the rest of its life	✔	✔ (times 9)	
— Can hygienically go "poop" without waking you in the middle of the night		✔	
— Has a distinct sense of smell	✔		
— Has a distinct smell			✔
— Would prefer that the entire house smelled like fish		✔ *	

*So will you when you get a load
of that distinct baby smell

During these first few weeks, it's a good idea to baby-proof your house. The basic baby-proofing elements are baby locks, electric outlet caps and a brick.

Baby locks are to be installed on drawers and cupboards where you keep household items (poisons, sharp objects, hand grenades) that might harm your baby. After these latches are installed, you're going to go through a period of adjustment getting used to the new way you have to open your cupboards. Unfortunately, until you've mastered this procedure, the cupboards are going to snap back on your fingers, resulting in severe sprains, abrasions and bleeding. This is extremely painful and will require some quick first aid. So, you'll run to your medicine cabinet — only to smash your fingers again because this too is baby-latched. This is where the brick comes in.

After you've cleaned up all the broken mirror glass, it will be time to install the electric outlet caps. These simply plug right into any electric outlet and are very difficult to pry out. You, of course, will have no trouble, thanks to the convenient splints on your fingers, compliments of the baby locks.

Some time between the first minute and the first month after you bring baby home, you're going to get lots of phone calls. Friends and relatives on the other end will ask how you and your baby are doing. When you hear this question, just say "fine". Repeat . . . just say "fine". Because, if you give the slightest clue that you or your baby are not "fine", you're in for a fate worse than birth. You're in for . . . *ADVICE!*

"WHATEVER YOU DO,
DON'T BELIEVE
THAT OLD WIVES' TALE
ABOUT SOAKING A
WASHCLOTH IN WHISKEY."

"CHICKEN SOUP.
THAT'S THE
BEST REMEDY FOR
DIAPER RASH."

BLAH!
BLAH!

"YOU'VE GOT TO LET
HER CRY FOR AT LEAST
4 HOURS STRAIGHT!"

"LET ME TELL YOU
WHAT AUNT EMMA
AND I DID FOR YOUR
COUSIN ELMER WHEN
HE HAD TYPHOID FEVER . . ."

YAK!
YAK!

"DON'T SPEND MONEY
ON THOSE BABY TOWELETTES,
JUST MOISTEN SOME
ZIG-ZAGS."

"LET HIM GUM
A WASHCLOTH
SOAKED IN WHISKEY."

For some reason, whenever new parents bring home a new baby, everybody in the world feels it's their calling in life to give the parents advice. Nobody ever gives you advice while you're pregnant — but carry a new baby into your entry way and — <u>BAM</u>! It's advice-o-matic! Of course, the most advice comes from two "expert" groups: (1) Grandparents, and (2) People With No Children. Ironically, these two factions are capable of giving you totally opposite opinions on every subject regarding your child. For every crisis that arises, Grandparents over-react — no harm should ever come to their little loved one. People With No Children, however, take a more hard-line approach. They'll have no "wimps" growing up in your family. The chart below illustrates these differences.

Crisis	Advice From Grandparents	Advice From People With No Children
Baby is crying.	Rush baby to the hospital.	Spank baby for making so much noise.
Baby won't breastfeed.	Rush baby to the hospital.	Give baby a frozen dinner.
Baby's diaper is full of poop.	Rush baby to the hospital.	Rub baby's nose in it to discourage this behavior in the future.

It's due to these irreconcilable differences of opinion that People With No Children will not even consider becoming Grandparents.

CHAPTER 5

Feeding Baby

How you will initially feed your baby is totally up to you. The choices are obvious: breast, bottle or McDonald's.

If you decide that baby is to be breastfed, then feeding baby is mommy's chore. When baby wakes in the middle of the night, it's mommy's responsibility to get up and administer the feeding. (Dads, the key phrase here is "middle of the night". Encourage your wife to breastfeed for as long as possible — say, seven to ten years. That should get you plenty of rest.)

So, Mom, while daddy's resting, here are a couple of things you should know about breastfeeding and its advantages:

— Breastfeeding is supposed to be the best form of nutrition for your baby, giving it a good start in life. Mother's milk contains all the necessary vitamins and minerals, and helps a baby's body grow in many different ways. In short, breast milk is almost as healthy as Wonder Bread.

— Breastfeeding is also convenient. You don't have to make frantic trips to the store, there's nothing to refrigerate, and, unless you belong to some strange cult, you don't have to spend time boiling any nipples.

Here are a couple of disadvantages:

— At some point, your baby is going to develop a few teeth. You will definitely be the first to know.

— If baby misses a feeding or two, your breasts are going to grow to about 15 times their already bigger-than-bearable size. This means the next time you bend over, you're going to be stuck in that position until help arrives.

If (or when) you decide to bottle-feed your baby, dads have to help out. Although it seems relatively simple, bottle feeding can be awkward the first time you attempt it. Mommy will probably do okay if she played with dolls when she was young. She'll have an almost sixth sense about bottle feeding. But when daddy was young, he probably never held anyone's head in the crook of his elbow unless he had some kid in a headlock during a fight. And, unless that kid was sucking on a bottle at the time, it's safe to assume that daddy has had very little experience in this area.

So, Dads, here are a few helpful hints to get you on your way when it's time to bottle-feed your baby:

— **Make sure you're holding baby right-side up.** This may sound a bit elementary, but sometimes, in the wee hours of the morning, you could be a little foggy. You must realize that the only way you're going to satiate baby's hunger is to be sure that you've got the bottle's nipple in the baby's mouth — and nowhere else.

— **Make sure you put formula in the bottle.** Again, at 2:00 a.m., this could be an oversight. Here are a few tell-tale signs that you're giving baby an empty bottle: baby's eyes will begin to cross; baby's right and left cheeks will come together inside its mouth; baby's tummy will inflate to the size of a beachball. If these signs lead you to believe that you forgot to put formula in the bottle — DO NOT REACT TOO QUICKLY! If you yank the suctioned bottle from the baby's mouth, you will send baby flying around the room bouncing off the walls and ceiling. This will not help baby's already crabby disposition.

— **Develop extremely quick head-and-neck reflexes.** When baby is finished feeding, you must put it over your shoulder to coax a burp. After baby has burped, it will then lean back, give you a contented, innocent-eyed look and project a stream of regurgitation with the speed equalled only by a major league fastball. Your ability to adroitly dodge this projectile will save your face from a disgusting experience. But plan on washing your walls about three times daily.

If your reflexes aren't that quick (or, at the other extreme, you've given yourself whiplash), you're going to need a spit-up cloth. Different types are shown below.

IMPRACTICAL   PRACTICAL

At some point, it'll be time to advance your baby to "solids". You'll know it's time when you go to lift baby out of its crib for breast or bottle feeding, and it's holding a plastic knife and fork.

"AIRPLANE-INTO-THE-HANGAR" GAME

The first time you feed solids to your baby, it's recommended that you don't leave the jar of baby food on the baby's table or high chair. Out of sheer curiosity, baby will try to knock that jar off to see if it will bounce, crack, shatter or explode. After 10 minutes of this behavior, you'll begin to develop the same curiosity about your baby's head.

Also, when you try to feed baby, things are obviously going to get a bit messy. A helpful suggestion is to dress baby in a vinyl raincoat to accommodate all the food that's going to dribble out of its mouth. (NOTE: If you're going to try to force that "smiling baby" spinach down your kid's throat, *you* had best wear a raincoat as well. In fact, open an umbrella.)

A "final approach" is the old airplane-into-the-hangar routine. This is where the spoon is the airplane — baby's mouth, the hangar. But, babies figure out your motive in a real hurry, making you circle the "airport" for a couple of hours. In a last-ditch effort, appeal to the control tower, telling your baby that there are lots of babies in its tummy anxiously awaiting the arrival of their mommies and daddies on your plane. Reluctantly, baby will open its mouth, accepting the spoon. To get even, however, baby will immediately shuttle the passengers out Gate Number 2.

CHAPTER 6

Pee-Pee And Poo-Poo

Most people have the misconception that all day long, the only thing a baby does is wet its diapers. This, of course, is not true. A baby makes "dirty" in its diapers, too. Believe it or not, that's a real "plus". Because the alternative is for the baby to "dirty" *not* in its diaper. Then, you're not going to need a diaper service — you'll need a janitorial service. Or disposable carpeting.

Okay, the subject's out in the open. Now, if you're one of those people who is going to hold your nose when changing a baby's diaper, you'd better close your eyes when reading this chapter because it's going to address the unpleasantries of urinary excretions and bowel movements — more commonly referred to by professionals as "pee-pee" and "poo-poo".

Contrary to popular belief, the elimination of food intake is not the sole reason that babies do pee-pee and poo-poo. Many top-notch doctors hold the view that babies "pee-and-poo" because it gives them a sense of accomplishment and a positive self-image. They note that many famous people — Einstein, Michelangelo, Joan Collins — all started out this way. Yet, more than a handful of psychologists have reasoned that pee-pee and poo-poo is your baby's way of getting back at you ahead of time for all the grief you're going to give it later about cleaning up its room.

Regardless of the actual reason, you're still going to have to deal with it. And the first thing you must do is think long and hard about how you're going to clean those messy diapers.

Now that you've decided that *you're* not going to clean those messy diapers (that decision really wasn't so long and hard after all), you have two choices:

1. Diaper Service. A good, economic option. However, many people don't like the ten-day wait between pick-up and delivery required by many of these services. But, there's good reason for this delay: It's the result of a covert operation being run in the name of "democracy".

THE FOLLOWING INFORMATION
IS TO BE SEEN BY ONLY
THOSE PEOPLE WHO
ARE CONSIDERING USING
DIAPER SERVICES.

THIS IS DEFINITELY

TOP
SECRET!

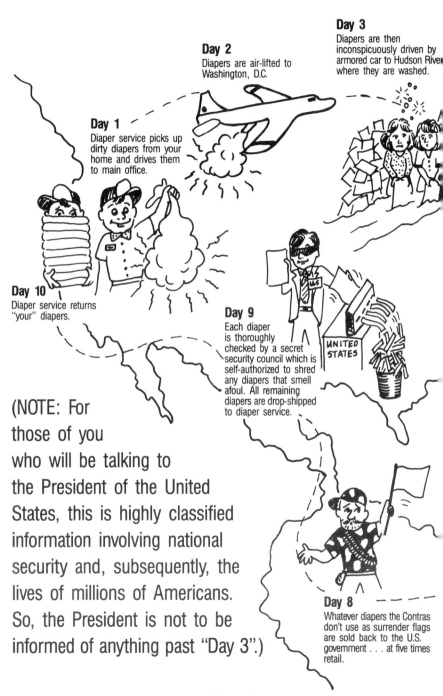

Day 3
Diapers are then inconspicuously driven by armored car to Hudson River where they are washed.

Day 2
Diapers are air-lifted to Washington, D.C.

Day 1
Diaper service picks up dirty diapers from your home and drives them to main office.

Day 10
Diaper service returns "your" diapers.

Day 9
Each diaper is thoroughly checked by a secret security council which is self-authorized to shred any diapers that smell afoul. All remaining diapers are drop-shipped to diaper service.

UNITED STATES

(NOTE: For those of you who will be talking to the President of the United States, this is highly classified information involving national security and, subsequently, the lives of millions of Americans. So, the President is not to be informed of anything past "Day 3".)

Day 8
Whatever diapers the Contras don't use as surrender flags are sold back to the U.S. government . . . at five times retail.

38

Day 4
Wet diapers are then sent
by overnight mail to Tehran.

Day 5
Iranian radicals dry the diapers
by wearing them on their heads
during daylight hours.

Day 6
Diapers sent to Israel, which
constantly complains that
diapers need to be
re-washed.

Day 7
Israel hires missionary plane
to smuggle repackaged
diapers into Nicaragua, which
buys them at wholesale.

2. Disposable Diapers. A much simpler approach. Just go to the store, pick out what you need and throw them away when you're done. When buying disposable diapers, you need to select the proper package to suit your baby. The package might indicate "up to 9 lbs." or "up to 16 lbs." For you neophytes, this refers to your baby's weight — not the diaper's holding capacity. Parents who are unaware of this may wonder why every time they take their baby out in public, people scamper off in the other direction, gagging and holding their hand over their nose and mouth. These same unaware parents also have babies who learn to walk much later in life than normal. It's not that their baby has deficient motor skills. It simply can't lift itself up.

You'll notice that disposable diapers give you several "baby" designs from which to choose. There's "Baby Mickey and Minnie", "Baby Kermit and Miss Piggy" and even a special collector's edition . . . "Baby Andy Gump".

Once you've selected the proper package, you must learn how to change baby's diaper. The first thing you have to do is find a convenient place to make the change. A bathroom, service porch or, depending upon the intensity, a toxic waste site will each provide adequate facilities.

It's safe to assume, for the moment, that you'll be doing this some place in your home. Diaper changing can be extremely messy and odoriferous, making you feel quite nauseous. But it doesn't have to be this way, especially if you follow the guidelines listed below:

1. Lay baby down.
2. Affix a clothespin to your nose.
3. Remove the diaper.
4. Sneak into your backyard and toss the diaper into your neighbor's yard.

Continue this procedure until the day you see your neighbor wearing a clothespin on *his* nose — approaching your front door — toting a shotgun.

It's just as critical to follow a certain routine when putting a new diaper *on* baby. You must be certain that the diaper's tape is securely fastened at baby's hips and that the elastic leg bands fit snugly around baby's thighs. If these two important steps are not thoroughly checked, and you're holding a baby who develops a nasty case of diarrhea, you're in for a real surprise — all over the front of your clothes. For this reason, it is strongly suggested that until you are quite adept at correctly putting a diaper on your baby, you don't wear *pullover* shirts.

Besides knowing *how* to change a baby's diaper, you have to know how *often*. Babies aren't always going

to let you know. You have to keep a mindful eye (or nose) on the situation. Here are some signs that will indicate you're not changing baby's diaper as often as you should:

— Your dog isn't *playing* dead.
— Jehovah's Witnesses only want to talk to you "through" your door.
— All your neighbors are wearing clothespins on *their* noses — and they're approaching your front door — pulling a cannon.

CHAPTER 7

How To Get Baby To Fall Asleep

Whether or not you realize it, you gave up a lot of things when you decided to have a baby: fun, freedom, romantic evenings, your virginity (unless you can get a few wise men to back your story), and, most of all, sleep.

You forfeited this pre-baby luxury because all the time when you normally would have been sleeping will now be spent trying to get your baby to sleep. This becomes a real tiresome task. Some babies just have a hard time falling asleep, which makes them cranky, making you cranky, making them crankier, making it even more difficult for them to fall asleep.

There are lots of theories on how to get a baby to fall asleep, and they all have one common denominator: None of them work. But, here are a couple of methods you might try when you've exhausted all the others.

Try taking baby for a ride in the car. This particular noise and movement should make baby very tired until it eventually nods off. So, it's important that *you* do the driving. Plus, if it's late at night (another daddy job), you should take two important preparatory steps:

1. Make sure your car has a full tank of gas.
2. Make sure your baby has recently been fed.

If these two steps are neglected, you could find yourself stranded miles from your home, wearing only a robe and slippers, frantically trying to flag down a "drive-around" mommy who can spare an extra gallon of gas from her car and 6-8 ozs. of milk from her breasts.

Singing to your baby can play an effective role in getting it to go "nite-nite". Although, if neither of you has a melodious voice, you might try following this simple procedure:

— Go to a record store.

— Pick up any Barbra Streisand album.

— When you get home, look at the record company's label.

— Call the record company and tell them that you'd like Ms. Streisand's home phone number so that you can call and ask that she make a personal appearance.

In case you get a snippy receptionist (or Barb wants too much money to do the "gig"), don't abandon the idea of a live performance. For a small donation and some hot cocoa, the local Salvation Army Band does a lovely rendition of "Brahms Lullaby".

Get Your Baby to Sleep with . . .

INSOMNIAC BABY GOLD!

Includes all the top lullabies for you and your baby to sing!

Featuring such all time classics as . . .

- *"Up, Up and Awake"* (5th Dimension)
- *"Rock Your Baby, Rock Your Baby, All Night Long"* (Steppenwolf)
- *Love Theme from "Rip Van Winkle"* (Mancini)
- *"Mel 'n Colic Baby"* (Tormé/Cocker)

Plus *A never-before released version of . . .*

"Voulez-Vous Couchez Avec un Pacifier?"
(Pia Zadora)

Don't Stay Awake a Minute Longer!
Order <u>Now!</u> Only $19.95!

YES! Please, I beg you, *<u>rush</u>* me "**Insomniac Baby Gold**" right away!!
Enclosed is my ☐ $20 cash   ☐ Signed blank check   ☐ Diamond watch
Just Please Hurry!!!

Check one: ☐ Album   ☐ Cassette   ☐ 8-Track*   ☐ Compact Disc

Name _____   Home Phone (___) _____
Address _____   Hours you can be reached ___24?___
City _____   Allow 4-6 weeks for delivery.
State _____ Zip _____   (So, drink lots of coffee for the time being.)

*Aren't you folks a little old to be having babies?

45

For the more serious cases, try something educational. See if you've got an old high school history book laying around. You may recall how, back in school, you'd have to read three chapters before the next morning. No sooner would you open the book, than you'd fall sound asleep. Begin reading this book to your baby and maybe it will have the same effect. If it does, baby will explain the three chapters to you when you awaken.

If you can't stand to read history, get out the vacuum cleaner. (Wasn't this some president's campaign slogan?)* Many times, the noise of a vacuum cleaner will put baby to sleep. Of course, it wakes up everybody else, but they can read your high school history book to solve that problem. A common theory attributed to the success of the vacuum method is that the noise it creates simulates the noise heard by the baby when it was in the womb. Therefore, the vacuum provides a familiar, comforting sound. If this "womb theory" is to "hold water", perhaps the two of you could simply scream at each other for about ten minutes. Your baby should recall that familiar noise and go directly to "Dreamland."

*(Yes, Hoover's.)

CHAPTER 8

How To Get A Baby To Stop Crying

If you firmly believe that you can get a baby to stop crying, you're either a hopeless optimist or deaf. As new parents, you must resign yourselves to the fact that your baby is going to cry. Because until your baby learns to say "Hey, you!", crying is its only way to get your attention.

A baby cries for many reasons. It could be frustrated, hurt, overtired or it may just want to go deep-sea fishing. It's your job to figure out the difference. Check its diaper. Check the moon. (Each of which could be "full".) Check the stock market (and keep a box of Kleenex handy for yourself). Discover the problem; then you can treat it.

Many parents, when they hear their baby cry, act on impulse and immediately feed the infant. This may be a big mistake. They don't even know if the baby is hungry. If this happens with *your* baby, don't jump to conclusions. Wait . . . and then, when you can no longer stand the screaming (this usually lasts up to three seconds), shove a breast or bottle into baby's mouth! Be advised, however, that this is a short-term solution only. You may be temporarily stifling the

47

noise level, but over the long run you'll be developing someone who will constantly whine and be grossly overweight. The positive side is that this same person will fit right in with about 92% of the American population.

Where a Baby's Cry Plots on the
"Loud Scale"

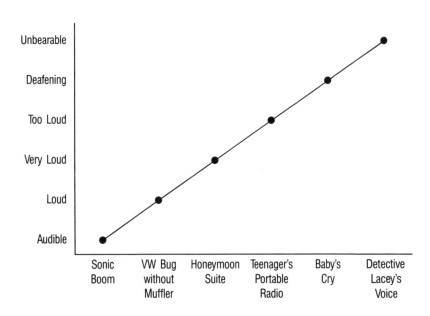

Your baby could be crying because it's teething. Ironically, about the only thing that hurts your kid's teeth more than having them pulled *out*, is having them push their way in. So, a teething baby is going to let you know about it . . . all night long. A soothing remedy is to let your baby bite down on something cold and plastic. (If you know any Hollywood agents, they can serve this role quite sufficiently.)

If your baby has a stuffy nose, it will become frustrated and begin to cry. Often, this makes its nose even more stuffy. Since a baby can't blow its nose, some pediatricians recommend that you clean baby's nostrils with a tiny bulb syringe. Realistically, this will take about a month and baby is not going to be real excited about the whole thing. Your goal is to clear that nasal swamp *fast* and stop the crying. So, get yourself a large turkey baster. (In fact, you'd better get two. This will save you from embarrassing questions at your next Thanksgiving dinner.)

A fussy baby who's persistently crying may not want to be touched or held. Don't even try. Instead, put a mirror in front of the baby. Many times babies will calm themselves by looking at their own reflections. If you don't have a mirror handy, an 8x10 color glossy of E.T. will be an adequate substitute. (You should have gotten one of these at your baby shower.)

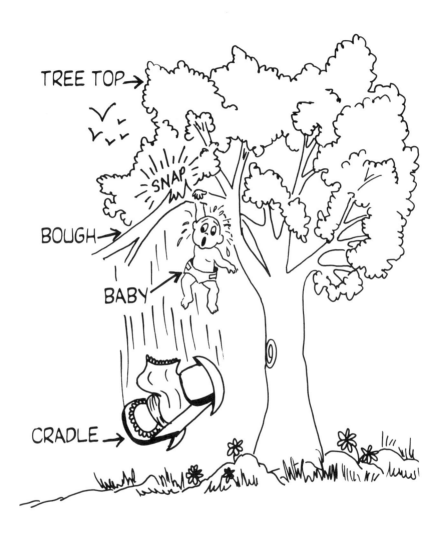

YET ANOTHER REASON A BABY CRIES.

Just as babies are intrigued by their likenesses, many will stop crying if they stare at a bright light. If your baby is crying in the middle of the night (daddy's job), and you don't feel like waking yourself up by turning on overhead lights and lamps, simply walk into your baby's room wearing a miner's helmet. The light from this should work just as effectively. If baby wakes up frequently throughout the night, you're not going to want to waste time fumbling around in the dark looking for the helmet. You can just keep it on each time when you return to bed. But don't forget to flick off the light — otherwise, you will greatly annoy your wife. This will do nothing to help your sex life. For some reason, a vast majority of women don't enjoy making love with a miner's light shining in their eyes all the while. This might explain why miners spend so much time in mines.

Last, but not least, baby could be crying because it's "spoiled". It's very difficult to spoil a new baby, but some parents may have unknowingly managed. If you suspect that this is the case with *your* baby, follow this simple procedure the next time it starts to cry. Sit down and make a quick list of everything you've done or gotten for your baby whenever it's cried in the past. When you're done, examine the list. If you see the word "Mercedes" anywhere, let the baby cry.

CHAPTER 9

Receiving Baby Gifts

After you've been home for a while, friends, relatives and acquaintances (who didn't attend your baby shower) will bring gifts for the newborn. These gifts will range from "wonderful" to "ridiculous". (Offering a night's worth of babysitting is "wonderful"; a cellular stroller phone is "ridiculous".)

Although everyone means well when they bring a gift, there's just no accounting for some people's taste. Common sense should dictate that if you bring home a baby boy, gifts should be in the blue family; conversely, if you bring home a baby girl, baby should receive something pink. It's that easy. Yet, some people insist on bringing gifts in hideous colors that don't match anything in baby's room, much less the garage where it's more likely to wind up. True, if the gift were bought before the baby's gender was known, these people might not have wanted to go with "blues" or "pinks" for fear of guessing incorrectly. But they could've just as easily gotten something in a nice neutral color. A tan cashier's check for $500 is an excellent example that would complement almost any decor. This type of thoughtfulness toward color scheme requires a special "thank you" on your behalf — like quickly spending the money on lots of foolish things for baby. If you're the type who's inclined to "put the money away for baby's education", forget it. By the time your brainchild is ready for Harvard, that $500 won't cover the cost of a "Pee-Chee" folder.

For those of you who didn't have a baby shower before baby's birth, it's in vogue to have a gift-giving get-together *after* your baby is born. Feel free to invite whomever you wish, so long as their adjusted gross income exceeds $70,000. These people will spend lots of money on your baby, assuring you of extra cash in your pocket when you return all of their gifts.

With the crowd gathered around, you'll be able to begin opening presents. As a concerned parent, the *safety* of each gift is now almost as important as the color. Without looking suspicious, or embarrassing anyone, conduct the following "baby gift safety test" as you open each present:

1. Chew on the gift.
2. Attempt to put the gift at least 2/3 the way up your nose.
3. Try to drive the gift through your forehead. (NOTE: If the gift is a bowling ball, in fairness to others, you should refrain from Step #3 until you've opened all of their gifts.)

Some people will give a special gift: Something they've made. This type of gift is truly from the heart — or, more likely, from the closet, so they can dump the atrocious-looking blanket one of their friends made for *their* baby. Nevertheless, *somebody* put a lot of time and effort into making this present, and it should be regarded as special. Make sure that the "giver" sees this gift in use whenever she comes over. Unless its use is as a drop cloth.

Regardless of the gift you receive, you're going to have to send out "thank you" notes. It's not always easy to write these without sounding trite or mundane, so on the next page is an "all-purpose" thank-you note that will allow you to personalize each message. What's more, these will be in your baby's words. If you really liked the gift, write the note using column "A". If you felt the gift was marginal, use only column "B". Or, if the gift was "el stinko", feel free to use column "C". You can also use any combination (there are 6,561 possible "thank yous") by mixing and matching columns.

(NOTE: For those chintzy folks who "went in" on a gift, return the favor by sending them a "thank you" chain letter.)

Dear (gift-giver's name),

	A	B	C
(1)	lovely	so-so	cheap
(2)	try it	trade it	trash it

Thank you for the ___(1)___ gift. I expect to ___(2)___ the first chance I get. I will always think of you whenever I ___(3)___ .

| (3) | play with it | see a nicer one | poop in my diaper |
| (4) | so nice | tacky | downright rude |

It was ___(4)___

of you to ___(5)___

| (5) | come over | ring the doorbell | drop in at dinnertime |
| (6) | spend the day | leave the gift on the front porch | stuff your face like a pig |

and ___(6)___ .

Anyway, thanks again, and I hope ___(7)___ .

| (7) | to see you soon | you still have the receipt | you're not invited to my first birthday |
| (8) | Love | Sincerely | Take a hike |

___(8)___ ,

___(baby's name)___

(optional if only column "C" was used)

CHAPTER 10

Finding A Babysitter

At some point (all new parents try this) you're going to attempt something stupid. The two of you are going to try to go out — without taking your baby. This heretofore unthinkable thought will cause you grave concern because, up until now, you haven't even gone to the bathroom without taking your baby.

The only way you'll be able to slightly relieve your apprehension is to find a competent babysitter. Of course, there are no competent babysitters. You'll have to settle for something else. (Perhaps you can locate a conscientious watchdog who can dial "9-1-1".)

Before you hire just "anybody", think about potential babysitters in your immediate area. Is there anyone in your neighborhood whom you would trust to watch your baby for an hour or so? If the answer is "no", consider moving. You're obviously living in the midst of a bunch of no-good low-lifes. Certainly there's another family with a young mother whom you could depend on to sit with your baby. Maybe you could work out a reciprocal arrangement: One time, *she* comes over to *your* house while *you* go out; the next time, *you* bring your baby over to *her* house while *you* go out. (If you can pull this off, start playing poker with this buffoon tomorrow.)

GRANDPARENTS BABYSIT FOR FREE(?)

Grandparents are a natural choice and they'll most likely babysit for free. But, as a rule, they can't see, hear or smell anything. When you return home and ask how things went, they can't remember either. You get what you pay for.

Another approach would be to look in your newspaper's classified section. There, you'll find many listings of women who advertise babysitting services. But, if you call any one of these women, qualify her carefully. Make sure she understands English — unless of course, you don't (in which case, you must find this book real interesting). Ask her what experience she has had with babies. If she tells you that she has twelve kids of her own, that only means she's experienced in *having* babies. Thank her very much and tell her that the next time you're thinking about conceiving, you'll hire her as a consultant.

You might find willing babysitters at the local high school. High school girls love to babysit. It gives them a chance to earn extra money while running up somebody else's phone bill. Here, again, you must carefully evaluate anyone you're considering hiring. Ask questions like:

— Do you know how to take a baby's temperature?
— Do you know how to change a baby's diaper?
— Do you intend to blast my stereo all night long?
— Do you know what the Prussians did to teen-aged girls who were commissioned to watch other people's children — and *failed*??
(This last one is a fabricated question, but, when asked in a stern, rhetorical fashion, it should sufficiently deter any thoughts about touching your stereo.)

Other questions you might ask can give you some insight into the girl's interests. This will allow you to prepare certain things that will make her babysitting experience more enjoyable. For instance, if you discover that she's into "fitness", buy a Nautilus machine and put it in the baby's room. This will keep her happy and allow her to keep an eye on your baby at the same time. If the girl is into "fatness", put a refrigerator in the baby's room — and stock it with junk food containing high levels of sugar. She'll be in "hog heaven" and this food will do an excellent job of keeping her awake. Unfortunately, it will also do an excellent job of keeping her fat. But, that's not your problem. She was fat *before* she got to your house.

When you're finally ready to make the move — and actually walk out the door — there will understandably be some uncertainty about leaving your baby with this stranger. You can allay these fears by arranging for a neighbor or the local SWAT team to periodically drop by.

Regardless of the type of babysitter you hire, you'll know you've picked the wrong one if:

— She doesn't page you every eight minutes at the restaurant to tell you everything is okay.

— She *does* page you every eight minutes at the restaurant — but you told her you'd be at the theater.

— You come home and discover a note explaining how she left two hours ago because "your baby woke up crying" and she "just isn't good in pressure situations".

— She is such a strong believer in the American economic system that the two dollars an hour you've been paying her over the past calendar year she reports as income and somehow the IRS takes notice and decides to come after you for not withholding any taxes from her earnings and consequently they audit your entire tax return and you wind up losing your house and cars and all your possessions and she tells you that if the two of you ever need a babysitter while you're in jail — she's available.

CHAPTER 11

Taking Baby To The Pediatrician

Remember when you were in grade school and occasionally you'd have a substitute teacher? The entire class could do whatever it wanted and not be punished. Flinging books at random heads, stabbing the person in front of you with a sharpened pencil, spitting at any girl who was wearing black and red on Friday, pulling hair, running around and screaming like banshees. In general, plain ol' obnoxious behavior.

This remembrance will instantly click when you open the door to the pediatrician's waiting room for the first time. Only, with these kids, it's worse. These kids are sick. But why are they allowed to wreak havoc upon everyone in this waiting room? There's a simple explanation for this.

No kid wants to be here in the first place. Most are deathly afraid of the doctor. Chances are good that the parents had to bribe their child just to get him to show up. So, when a child is misbehaving in the doctor's waiting room, what's the parent supposed to do? — say, "If you don't stop that this instant, we're going right home!"? That's the kid's perfect "out". Threats don't work in the pediatrician's waiting room. Anarchy prevails.

As you stand in the doorway with your baby, peering in at these runny-nosed, coughing, sneezing, scratching, screaming brats, you'll have serious doubts about going in. After all, you're liable to leave this place in worse condition than when you arrived. Don't worry. Just enter the room as inconspicuously as possible. AND DON'T TOUCH ANYTHING! It's all contaminated with germs. (Plastic reptiles and *Highlights* magazines are definite "hands off" material.) Very slowly, just cover your baby and go stand in a corner behind the potted plant. (Tall ferns and ficus trees provide adequate protection from spitballs and other lightweight flying objects. Be smart. Check with your pediatrician beforehand to see if these types of plants already exist in his waiting room. If not, you can bring your own — or interview other, more concerned pediatricians.)

When it is your baby's turn to see the doctor (usually about two hours or 86 medical forms after your scheduled appointment, whichever comes first), you'll be able to enter the more sane confines of the examining room — where you'll easily wait another half hour. But, you can use this time wisely.

Look around.

You can learn a lot about your pediatrician just by studying this room. Does he have something more impressive than a correspondence school diploma hanging on the wall? Are there indications of good-luck charms on the shelves? Are there bullet holes in the window?

Look around.

At this point, one of the nurses will come in to take care of some preliminary work. She'll weigh your baby, measure its length and measure the circumference of its head. This is to determine your baby's hat size so they can try and sell you a cute bonnet on your way out.

When the doctor finally arrives, your baby will sense his mere presence and start screaming at the top of its lungs. The doctor (with hands over ears) will look at what the nurse wrote down, spend about 20 to 30 seconds checking over your baby and deliver a well-founded diagnosis. If your baby is well, the doctor will quickly dismiss you and tell you to schedule another appointment for next month. If your baby is *not* well, the doctor will then begin to rattle off some medical terminology (usually extremely high in Latin content) and write you a prescription. If you're smart, you'll ask about the safety of this medicine. Rather than bore you with more "doctor talk" that you wouldn't understand, the doctor will merely give you the all-assured line, "I gave it to *my* kids." That's fine. But, if you wanted parental advice, you'd have consulted some People With No Children. (See page 28.) You're here for medical

YOU CAN LEARN A LOT BY LOOKING AROUND
YOUR PEDIATRICIAN'S EXAMINING ROOM.

DON'T ACCEPT
A PRESCRIPTION
WITHOUT ASKING
ABOUT SIDE EFFECTS.

advice. Ask the doctor what happened when he gave this medicine to his kids. What he may not be telling you is that his daughter grew warts on her forehead, dropped out of the third grade and joined a motorcycle gang. So, when your pediatrician prescribes something, don't be afraid to ask questions like, "If I give this to my daughter, will she grow warts on her forehead, drop out of the third grade and join a motorcycle gang?" If the doctor looks at you strangely, as if you have just insulted his years of experience and professional integrity, and then avoids giving you a straight answer, it immediately explains two things:

1. Some other, less inquisitive parents didn't ask that question and their daughter did acquire those traits.
2. The bullet holes in the window.

CHAPTER 12

Travelling With Baby

One of the most overlooked items when preparing for a newborn is the baby's car seat. If you've yet to purchase one and you gave birth a couple of weeks early, you've probably suffered the embarrassment of having to leave your baby at the hospital while you scavenged the newspapers watching for a sale. If you're thinking about trying to get baby home *without* a car seat (shipping UPS is not advisable), you may choose one of the following methods:

— **Bicycle.** Simply put baby on the back of bike and you're off! (NOTE: Please remember — no "wheelies".)

— **Have an elderly person drive you and baby in one of those "electric" cars.** This is only acceptable if you don't mind your baby being four years old by the time you get home.

— **Put on a pair of ruby slippers, hold baby under your arm, click your heels three times and say repeatedly, "There's no place like home."** Then pray you don't wind up in Kansas.

Many states require by law that any time you take a baby in the car it must be properly secured in a car seat. These "protective" devices range from the inexpensive type — an inflatable booster seat with a bungi cord — to the more costly but more sturdy type — made of molded plastic. There's even a rather practical model with a built-in potty seat in case baby has an accident immediately after you do. Some adults could use this feature as well.

Placement of the car seat is very important. Child safety experts suggest that you position the car seat in the center of your car's back seat. This is so baby is not sitting dangerously close to a door's window where glass could shatter during an accident. There are two other, and perhaps equally important, reasons for center-seat placement:

1. It makes it more difficult for baby to reach over and roll down a window where it can "moon" other drivers.

2. The center of the back seat is the optimum position for baby to listen to your car stereo. In fact, in a recent survey among babies in car seats, an astonishing 78% reported that The Who's rock opera, "Tommy" was outstanding when heard from the car's center back seat position. (Ironically, only 2.7% voted for Fisher-Price's "Greatest Hits".) So there you have it.

Once you've gotten baby strapped into the car seat (this will take about 3-4 hours the first time you try it), you're on your way.

Where do you think you're going? None of your friends are going to invite you over. They don't want that screaming "meemie" in their house. You'd do better by choosing a place where babies are accepted, if not wanted . . . like:

— **The Zoo.** This cultural outing will give your baby a chance to experience the exotic sights and smells of foreign creatures. And these are just the visitors.

— **The Ballgame.** Here you can acquaint your baby with loudmouths screaming obscenities, aromatic cigar smoke, nitrate-ridden hot dogs and other touches of Americana. But, unless you want to pay for an extra seat, you'll have to hold baby on your lap. This could present quite a problem if you're also trying to balance a few *beers* on your lap. Suppose a foul ball is headed your way. You have to make an instantaneous decision: Drop the beer? Drop the baby? Considering the wait in line to get another beer, this could be a tough choice — especially for Cub fans. (Yankee fans can avoid this dilemma by quickly handing the baby to their parole officer.)

— **The Post Office.** This can be a real confidence-builder for baby if you follow these simple steps: Bring a letter and get in line. When it's your turn, take baby to the window. Have baby drool all over the stamp and slap the stamp anywhere onto the envelope. Then, let baby throw the envelope any which way. Baby is now qualified to get a job here.

— **The Restaurant.** Bringing a baby into a

posh restaurant means never having to make a reservation. Just walk in with the screaming infant and the place will empty out as if someone had just yelled "Fire!". You'll have the table of your choice. This, of course, will not set well with the maitre d', but don't take any lip. Threaten to eat at his establishment *every* night. (NOTE: If offered a booster seat, do **not** accept it. This will only make your baby's head an easier "mark" for baked potatoes, large meatballs and other culinary mortar shells lobbed by die-hard patrons.)

Some parents get real brave and take their baby on an airplane. If you decide to try this, it's a good idea to check ahead of time with two or three airlines to ask some important questions:

— **"What's the movie?"** You'll prefer one that you've already seen . . . since you're not going to get a chance to watch this one.

— **"How many carry-on things can I bring on the plane?"** This is crucial to know because, if you're ready to board and you've got more than the allowable number of carry-ons, your baby is going to have to ride with the luggage. This guarantees that you and your baby will wind up in different cities.

— **"Do you have a 'Frequent-Crier' program?"** Many airlines, in an attempt to attract the new-parent-with-baby travellers, offer these types of incentive programs.

FREQUENT-CRIER PROGRAM	
When Every Flight is a "Red-Eye"	
If Your Baby Cries For	You Receive
10,000 miles	Complimentary headset to block out the noise.
50,000 miles	Free upgrade to first-class while baby remains with the cheap passengers.
100,000 miles	Lifetime pass for you and your baby on another airline. Enough's enough.

Also, check with the airlines regarding their diaper-changing policies. The fancier lines will have a flight attendant take your baby and change the diaper for you. The majority, however, adhere strictly to an FAA regulation that requires anyone changing a dirty diaper to store it in an overhead compartment or under the seat in front of them. If *you* do this, you'll notice

that, in a very short time, the entire cabin is going to reek. Unfortunately, there's another FAA regulation (and maybe one that needs amending) which states that at least three passengers have to be lying unconscious in the aisles before oxygen masks can be released. Perhaps the best policy is offered by the "no-frills" airlines, which pay no attention to the FAA and merely have you throw the dirty diaper out an emergency exit at the appropriate moment. Like when the plane is passing over New Jersey.

Finally, it's very important that your baby has a good experience on its maiden flight, so you should take precautionary action to assure your baby's comfort and safety. Before take-off, go into the cockpit and show the co-pilot your seat number; and ask him to put a "Baby on Board" sticker outside your window. This will alert other DC-10s, 747s and the like to be courteous (e.g., not to bump into your plane or make a lot of noise by revving their engines) when flying in your airspace.

CHAPTER 13

Increasing Your Baby's Intelligence

Back in the '50s and '60s, parents were developing their babies' grey matter by letting them play with blocks and flashcards. Consequently, when this baby boom bunch of "blockheads" and "flashers" became adults, they were super-intellectuals who could talk circles around anyone when discussing the alphabet (A-to-Z) and numbers (1-to-10).

Certainly times have changed and today's parents realize that they can no longer teach their babies using these same blocks and flashcards — mainly because they've lost them all. Today's parents must find more ingenious ways to educate their babies.

You should be working at this from the moment your baby is born. During the bonding process, you should be explaining the Pythagorean Theorem, comparing and contrasting the socio-economic system instituted by the Incas to that of the white-collared Pilgrims and playing the home version of "Jeopardy". Because, if your baby learns nothing now, you're going to have to pay tons of money to send it to college for the same result *later*.

If you do aspire (for some unknown reason) to send your kid to college some day, you must begin at the earliest possible time to stress the importance of brainpower. Without brainpower, your baby will have no chance to get through the educational system. Dinosaurs are the perfect example. Dinosaurs ruled the earth. They had giant bodies, sabre-like teeth, sharp talons and huge, powerful heads . . . but very tiny brains. As a result, none of these behemoths ever attended a major university. Of course, this was before football scholarships were big business.

You see, if your baby can get through college, it has a chance to go on to become a doctor. As everybody knows, doctors make a lot of money by using words that nobody can figure out. Evidence of this is found in "The Cat in the Hat Comes Back" and "How the Grinch Stole Christmas", available in any (except medical) library.

It's important to let your baby explore. Give it things to hold and feel. Hand baby a globe, from which it can learn a lot. Not only will baby be able to study all the different countries and their relative geographic locations, but when the globe drops and shatters into thousands of pieces, baby will acquire an immediate understanding of nuclear physics.

If you're one of the lucky few, you may have the opportunity to enroll your newborn in the "Pre-School

for Gifted Babies". Not just anyone can get into this school. (You must be tall enough to reach the doorknob.) The program will only accept babies who have passed the pre-school pre-entrance exam. This exam covers a wide range of questions from math, political science, economics, biology, English, music and other subjects your child probably will not learn about in later schooling. To help your baby prepare for this pre-school pre-entrance exam, following are some sample questions and answers that will be on the test. Drill your baby (in a manner of speaking). Make sure your baby knows these answers like the back of its hand — which is, incidentally, a good place to put them just before baby takes the exam.

Q. If a baby starts off at the size knee-high to a chromosome, and grows to be about 4.5 million times that size while still in the womb, then, during labor, passes through the birth canal at a rate of 2.5 centimeters per hour for 27 hours, what is the maximum decibel level that mommy can reach while screaming?

A. No one knows for sure, but it's loud enough so that mommy and daddy will not have to send birth announcements to anyone living within a five-mile radius of the hospital.

Q. Why do presidential candidates kiss babies?

A. Kissing "babes" is good "P.R." for those who run for the presidency. (Unless your name is Gary Hart.)

Q. Are there babies on other planets?

A. To date, we have no reason to believe that there is intelligent life on other planets. Furthermore, judging from the amount of earthlings who continue to have babies, there is little sign of intelligent life on *this* planet as well.

Q. What effect does the Beatles' music have on today's babies?

A. The Beatles are blamed by a baby's grandparents for creating a generation of kids (the baby's parents) who just sat around listening to drug-inducing, sexually-explicit music known as "rock and roll"; and for all the other things in life that are bad. Except for ugliness. For this, they blame Mick Jagger.

Q. If a baby has five stinky poops a day, and, after each poop, daddy sneaks out of the room so that mommy has to change the diaper, how many total diapers will daddy have to change over the course of the next six months?

A. None. It's impossible to change a diaper while in traction.

Q. Why does a baby get cold feet?

A. Before baby is born, both mommy and daddy have paying jobs; but *after* baby is born, only one of them has a paying job. This means that mommy and daddy have to eat baby's shoes for dinner.

Q. From time to time, you may hear your mommy and daddy referred to as "yuppies". Explain what this means.

A. Yuppies are people who drive BMWs, wear designer clothing and live in nice houses because they can afford it. Yuppies are also the people who, 20 years ago, were called "hippies" who condemned all of the above because they *couldn't* afford it.

Q. Why is daddy no help around the house?

A. Good question.

Before you set too high of a standard for your baby, remember that its intelligence is directly related to yours. Keep in mind that it was you and your spouse who put your heads together (as well as other anatomical parts) when you decided to have a baby in the first place. Soon, you'll see just how intelligent *that* was. Go easy on the kid.

PARENTS' INTELLIGENCE TEST

Since it has been proven that *your* intelligence has a direct effect upon your baby's potential "smarts", here's an opportunity to prove to the world that your kid is genius material. Below are five questions that will measure your intellect and your kid's chances of getting past "See Dick run."

1. In what year was the first household-like dwelling created?
2. Who did "Tiny Tim" marry on the "Tonight" show?
3. In 25 words or less, what is Elizabeth Taylor's full name?
4. Who weighs the most:
    a. William "Refrigerator" Perry?
    b. Arnold Schwarzenegger?
    c. "Hulk" Hogan?
5. What was Gracie Allen's fool-proof method for cooking a roast?

(Answers on next page)

ANSWERS TO PARENTS' INTELLIGENCE TEST

1. About 300,000 B.C. Sadly, nothing remains to truly document this structure's existence. Except for the stiffened body of a Neanderthal insurance salesman in what archaeologists believe to have been a doorway.

2. The correct answer is "Miss Vicki". The *better* answer is "Who cares?"

3. Elizabeth Taylor Hilton Wilding Todd Fisher Burton Burton Warner.
(NOTE: This answer is as of May 13, 1990, at three hours, forty-four minutes and seventeen seconds.)

4. Nell Carter.

5. Put a small roast and a large roast into the oven at the same time. When the small one is burned, the large one is ready.

Test Results

5 right — Your child will be brilliant — or a walking compendium of useless information.

3-4 right — Your child will breeze through school, never needing to do its homework. (Watch for your kid's reaffirmation of this when it turns 13 years old.)

1-2 right — Trouble sign. Your child will start out with a "bang", but will peak at long division. (Envious?)

0 right — Back to blocks and flashcards.

CHAPTER 14

Preparing For What Lies Ahead

As your baby begins to grow, you'll be in for all sorts of interesting challenges. Maintaining your mental stability is not the least of them. Every day will bring something new and something different. Below is a quick-reference-not-necessarily-chronological list of events that you can expect to encounter in the coming months.

— **Vocalizing.** This is the first sign of your baby's attempt to converse. There is no set age at which this will begin. Each baby will go at its own pace. For instance, Baby Howie Cosell was supposedly *born* shouting, "Did you see that? Did you see that? What a dexterous display of delivery by the man they call . . . the Doctor!" Whereas, it is chronicled that Baby Ronnie Reagan just smiled and said absolutely nothing for nearly eight years. Chances are that *your* baby will fall somewhere in between these two extremes. Remember, when your baby does begin to utter some sounds, while they may carry a similarity only to the Pakistani national anthem, your baby is trying to tell you something . . . like, "I love you" or "You have B.O." In either case, you'd want to know.

— **Taking Medicine.** This means war! No baby wants to take medicine and will fight you through every milliliter. And, flavoring is not the answer. All the baby has to see is a dropper filled with liquid and it's ready for battle. The trick is to outsmart your baby. Ask your pharmacist to mold the medicine in the form of "Lego's". Then leave one of these on your living room floor. Baby will automatically put this into its mouth and swallow it. Do this four times a day as needed.

— **Baby's First Christmas.** This is a "biggy". In some circles, it's right up there with baby's first steps or baby's first words. (If you're Jewish, the equivalent here is baby's first investment.)

— **Pulling the Dog's/Cat's Tail.** No preparation is sufficient for this. You can't stop it. But, it's only going to happen once. All you'll need is a long pole to induce your baby to come down from the ceiling.

— **Playing with the Telephone.** What starts out to be a playful lifting of the receiver off the hook turns out to be some expensive random button-pushing. Unless *you* made calls to Kenya and Irkutsk. If you must let baby play with the phone, have it do so after 5:00 p.m. on weekdays or anytime on weekends when random button-pushing is usually cheaper.

— **Dating.** You really don't have to worry about this quite so early, but keep in mind that whatever your baby does now may become habit later. There are some things you just don't want your kid doing on dates. Rubbing oatmeal all over its face, taking off its own poopy diaper and giving it a discus-like hurl across the room, and sucking its thumb (or anybody else's for that matter) are just a few of the habits you'll want to break by the prom.

— **Imitating.** This is where babies excel. They're better at this than mimes or monkeys. If you use four-letter words as part of your every-day vocabulary, your baby is going to use four-letter words as part of its every-day vocabulary. If you walk around your house in your underwear, eating Vienna sausages out of the can, your baby is going to walk around your house in its underwear, eating Vienna sausages out of the can. And on and on. In fact, this innate, involuntary ability to imitate is so strong that, when your parents tell you that the two of you make lousy parents — suddenly, it all makes sense!

— **Crawling.** Your baby's new-found mobility can prove advantageous to both of you. For the first time, baby can get around without your help. As a result, you can now send baby to the store (small grocery lists only). Interestingly, many babies learn to crawl backwards before crawling forwards. Therefore, make sure there's a store in either direction.

— **Tantrums.** Known to be the leading cause of vasectomies. Tantrums don't usually begin until your child turns two, at which point you can't wait until your child turns eighteen. There are three basic types of tantrums:

1. The "Kangaroo" Tantrum: Noted for its rapid jumping in place until the child begins to wear a hole in the floor. If you live in a two-story dwelling, do not get your kid upset while on the upstairs level.

2. The "Stop, Drop and Roll" Tantrum: Recognized by the sudden cessation of whining, a flinging of baby's body to the ground and a fast-paced rolling back and forth. Avoid getting your baby angry at all costs if it's in the backyard — and you have a dog.

3. The "Spearchucker" Tantrum: Anything that isn't nailed down becomes fair game. Ash trays, candy dishes and crystal decanters will fly through the air with the greatest of ease. Natural targets will be windows, television screens and your head. Therefore, it is highly recommended that you temporarily give up your expensive "decorator" taste and learn to live with "early Nerf".

— **Vasectomy.** (Another daddy job.) This is a difficult decision. The mere thought of it makes daddies feel a bit uncomfortable. This is really unwarranted. Vasectomies have come a long way in the past ten years. You can have it done as outpatient surgery and about 80% of them are "reversible". This means, when it's over, you can give one to the doctor if you like.

EPILOGUE

Watching my wife go through labor was one of the most difficult things I have ever experienced. I had to know when to be firm and when to be gentle. I had to know when she truly needed medical assistance and when it was just a passing pain. I had to be able to smile after taking a right cross to the chin and know when to restrain myself from hitting back. And, most of all, I had to shut up — because I was in the room with the only person in the world to whom I couldn't complain. My problems were miniscule compared to what she was going through.

After about 11 of what were to be 14 hours of labor, she began the period known as "transition". This is the part of labor when the pain says, "You ain't felt nothin' yet!" Her contractions got stronger and more frequent. With each one, it looked as if her eyes were going to pop off her face. (I know I must've looked the same to her as I struggled to remove her hands from my throat.)

As she lay on the bed with nothing to relieve this "natural child-bearing euphoria", except for an oxygen mask to prevent hyperventilation, one of the nurses skipped into the room to check out the dilation status. As if she were totally unaware of my wife's writhing in pain, the nurse, with all the gaiety of a candy-striper, asked, "So, do we have a name for this child?"

"Yes", my wife gasped. "Only."

(NOTE: Three and one-half years later our second child was born.)

And so it goes.

Paul R. Feininger

Your Baby's Diary

The following pages will help you to keep records of important "baby" events and information for your little one to cherish for years to come.

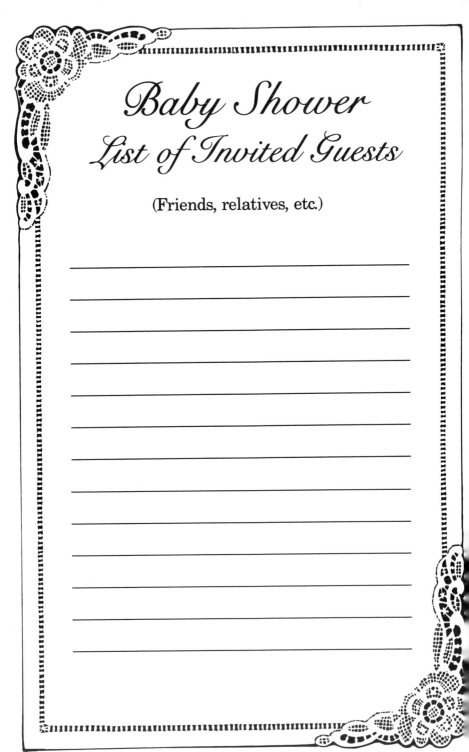

Baby Shower
List of Invited Guests

(Friends, relatives, etc.)

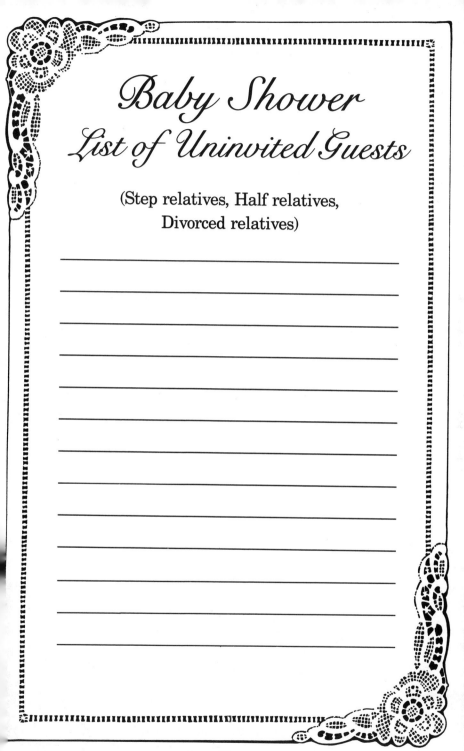

Baby Shower
List of Uninvited Guests

(Step relatives, Half relatives,
Divorced relatives)

_____

_____

_____

_____

_____

_____

_____

_____

_____

_____

_____

_____

_____

_____

Baby Shower
List of Guests who Brought Gifts Valued at Less than the Food You Served Them

(Enter from previous page)

_____

_____

_____

_____

_____

_____

_____

_____

_____

_____

Baby's Birth Statistics

*Weight*_____ (in pounds)

*Length*_____ (in inches)

*Doctor's Bill*_____ (in millions)

Baby's First Photograph

(NOTE: If baby is born in the Bronx,
use baby's first "Mug Shot".)

Affix Here

Baby's First Poop

(Don't even *think* of affixing that here!)

Phone Numbers Most Frequently Called

Pediatrician _____

Pediatrician _____

Pediatrician _____

Pediatrician _____

Pediatrician _____

Pediatrician _____

Pediatrician _____

Pediatrician _____

Pediatrician _____

Pediatrician _____

Pediatrician _____

Pediatrician _____

Pediatrician _____

Pediatrician _____

Pediatrician _____

Date Your Baby First Showed Interest in Your "Private Parts"

_____

Date Your Spouse Showed Renewed Interest in Your "Private Parts"

N/A

TITLES BY CCC PUBLICATIONS

—NEW BOOKS—

FOR **MEN** ONLY (How To Survive Marriage)

HORMONES FROM HELL (The Ultimate *Women's* Humor Book)

GIFTING RIGHT (How To Give A Great Gift Every Time! For Any Occasion! And On Any Budget!)

THE SUPERIOR PERSON'S GUIDE TO EVERYDAY IRRITATIONS

HOW TO TALK YOUR WAY OUT OF A TRAFFIC TICKET

YOUR GUIDE TO CORPORATE SURVIVAL

WHAT DO WE DO NOW?? (The Complete Guide For All New Parents Or Parents-To-Be)

—SPRING 1991 RELEASES—

THE Unofficial WOMEN'S DIVORCE MANUAL

HUSBANDS FROM HELL

HOW TO REALLY PARTY!!!

THE GUILT BAG [Accessory Item]

—BEST SELLERS—

NO HANG-UPS (Funny Answering Machine Messages)

NO HANG-UPS II

NO HANG-UPS III

GETTING EVEN WITH THE ANSWERING MACHINE

HOW TO GET EVEN WITH YOUR EXes

HOW TO SUCCEED IN SINGLES BARS

TOTALLY OUTRAGEOUS BUMPER-SNICKERS

THE "MAGIC BOOKMARK" BOOK COVER [Accessory Item]

—CASSETTES—

NO HANG-UPS TAPES (Funny, Pre-recorded Answering Machine Messages With Hilarious *Sound Effects*) — In Male or Female Voices

Vol. I: GENERAL MESSAGES

Vol. II: BUSINESS MESSAGES

Vol. III: 'R' RATED

Vol. IV: SOUND EFFECTS ONLY

Vol. V: CELEBRI-TEASE (Celebrity Impersonations)

Coming Soon:

Vol. VI: MESSAGES FOR SPORTS FANS